Poems by **Jane Yolen**

Illustrated by **Josée Masse**

THUNDER UNDERGROUND

WORDSONG

AN IMPRINT OF HIGHLIGHTS

Honesdale, Pennsylvania

For Alison Isabelle Stemple, a fine young poet and marvelous granddaughter, and for Rebecca Davis, whose editing of poetry is marvelous in its own right —JY

For my friends Marc and Hélène, with whom I love to share the adventures that life has to offer —JM

Acknowledgement:
"Subway" © 2004 by Jane Yolen, published in *Spider Magazine*.

Text copyright © 2017 by Jane Yolen
Illustrations copyright © 2017 by Josée Masse
All rights reserved.
For information about permission to reproduce selections from this book,
contact permissions@highlights.com.

WordSong
An Imprint of Highlights
815 Church Street
Honesdale, Pennsylvania 18431
Printed in China

ISBN: 978-1-59078-936-0
Library of Congress Control Number: 2016942425

First edition
Design by Barbara Grzeslo
Production by Sue Cole
The text of this book is set in Futura.
The drawings are done in mixed media.
10 9 8 7 6 5 4 3 2 1

CONTENTS

UNDER

–ground

Beneath our feet,
a world apart,
is found our Earth's
fast-beating heart.
It keeps us living,
soil and root,
while up above
we eat the fruit.

–stand

Knowledge grounds
a power base,
so seek out knowledge
touched by grace.
Start below,
reach for the sky,
and like the caterpillar
fly.

UNDER THE HOUSE

Here is a cellar,
a basement,
a clutter,
a helter-skelter,
a maze,
cables, pipes,
the basic foundation,
a storage,
a story,
the oldest page.

Read house history
in the Under.
Use imagination.
Wonder.

6

SEEDS

This dot,
this spot,
this period at the end
of winter's sentence
writes its way up
through the dull slate of soil
into the paragraph of spring.

CORNY CONVERSATIONS

In sounds too odd
for us to hear,
corn plants can talk,
not mouth to ear.
But with a strange
and clicking sound,
their taproots speak
beneath the ground.
We don't know what
corn rootlings say
when they communicate
this way.
But scientific studies
show
they do this as they
grow and grow
and grow.

THUNDER UNDERGROUND

Thunder
under-
ground.
That's
the sound
beetles make
when
walking
'round.
Squeaky
like a
creaky door,
clicking,
clacking,
muffled roar,
beetles on the
underfloor.
Scritch,
scratch,
scrunch,
that's
the crunch
of beetles
eating
beetle lunch—
all roots,
no punch.

10

OH, TO BE AN ANT

Oh, to be an ant,
neat, quiet, indifferent
to anything but constant work;
hurrying, scurrying, burying;
line after line,
their labors unceasing
from hill to hill,
always quiet,
                never
                        still.

Their mega-city
cambered, chambered,
tied by endless highways,
byways made by workers,
hauling dirt four times
their weight.
Not architected by one will,
but thousands working,
                    never
                        still.

EARTHWORM

Inch by inch,
and root by root,
the tiny earthworm crawls.
It makes its living
in the dirt
creating its own walls.

It oils those walls
for ease of passage,
gurgling as it goes;
a slime machine,
while all around it
things just decompose.

MOLE EATS

"A mole eats its own weight in
earthworms every twenty-four hours . . ."
—Lilo Hess

After a day of feasting,
the larder should be quite bare,
but mole does not worry.

He hoards his earthworms,
a thousand wriggly snacks
now stilled in his inky cupboards.

VELVET

"Live like the velvet mole . . ."
—Elinor Wylie

Mole in his hole,
the soft brown of old rubbed velvet,
wrinkles up dirt through the night.
Does he daydream of grass
or the roots of grass?
Does he listen to beetles passing?
Does he count in his blind way
the pink ribbony worms?
Or are his thoughts
dark and deep
as velvet tunnels,
velvet sleep?

SUBWAY

I like the sound the subway makes
deep in its underground den.
I like the growling as it goes
from street to street,
                     and then
I like the squeals its iron wheels
make coming 'round again.

I like the flickering lights below,
that make the night-time day.
I like the rumbling, jumbling cars
along the long railway.
I only wish that I could ride
the subway trains
                    all day.

UNDER THE CITY: TWO VIEWS

1.

Like mammoth moles who relentlessly tunnel
    drilling down,
    shoring up,
    filling,
    piling,
    hauling,
    mauling,
    cementing,
    tiling,
    we break,
    make,
    change,
    sunder,
bringing light to the dark down Under.

2.

Here in the black places of the world,
lie the noisy skirls of change:
lacings of pipes, snorkeling sewers,
skewers of bridge footings.
Here basements huddle in the dirt,
train platforms sulk within the earth.
Rats in the false night eat and play,
while cockroaches couch throughout the day.
Then true night calls them out to wonder,
For Up is now as black as Under.

17

THREE THINGS I KNOW ABOUT THE ROOTS OF TREES

1.
Roots are the tree's pantry,
its storage bin.
Larder, hoarder, not quite a rhyme,
but a reason.

2.
Three times the branches' spread,
roots fan out,
an underground portrait
of the tree above.

3.
Like Atilla and his hordes,
roots destroy the concrete culture,
crushing the modern with their
relentless barbaric blows.

LOST CITY

Long, long ago a home was lost,
a road, a city, a world was tossed,
into the trash, in history's dump,
covered with grass, an odd-shaped hump
that generations all forgot.

Trees grew tall, cows grazed, birds nested.
Young folk climbed the hill and tested
gravity's relentless pull,
picnicked on the top till full
on this odd, forgotten spot.

Archaeologists found the place
that tangled time and dirt erased.
With careful surveys, digging, scraping,
all in all, an odd landscaping,
they uncovered the city's plot.

They read the lie, they parsed the story—
rebuilt all the site's old glory.
By the time that they were through,
the tale became both old and new;
unraveled was the ancient knot.

PIRATE TREASURE

On the map
a bony finger
signals that
you must not linger.

Hidden in trunks
bolted tight
the gold doubloons stay
out of sight.

But follow quickly,
now you know
what treasure waits you
far below.

See? On the map,
X marks the spot.
Am I quite sure?
I Kidd you not.

NOTES FROM SOME OLD FOSSILS

Buried at sea,
Set me free.

Long bogged down,
In mud I drown.

Volcanic plunder
Way down under.

MAGMA POOLS

Hot, hot, hot,
In magma pools
Becoming rock
When magma cools.

So, should we wait
An Age or two
To see what magma pools
Can do?

I haven't got the time,
Have you?

TECTONIC PLATES: A HAIKU

Large table setting.
When the plates are moved around,
Continents can drift.

EARTH QUAKE

Ground shakes,
Remakes.
Mountains rise
Toward the skies.
Day dawns,
Earth yawns.
World is new.
What can we do?

UNDERGROUND RIVERS

Silver above,
black ribbon below,
twisting round roots,
the dark rivers go.

If nobody sees them
are they really there?
Only deep animals
seem to be ware.

SPELUNK

Go into the mouth
of a very large cave.
It will feel awfully much
like a dark and damp grave.

There are people who will not
spelunk on a bet
for it all sounds quite scary,
and dirty, and wet.
                    And yet . . .

Turn on your headlamp—
stone jewels everywhere.
Stalactites hang down,
so you have to take care.

Take a breath, take your time,
and look wonderingly around,
at the fairy-tale castles
so far underground.

UNDER

—stood

So now you know,
you've found, you care
what lies beneath
us everywhere:
roots and rootlings,
beetles, moles,
rivers rushing
through deep holes,
seeds and cellars,
subways, caves,
fossils, magma,
treasures, graves.

But mostly there's
Earth's fresh green heart,
with under-roots,
its secret part.
　　Where we all end.
　　And we all start.

NOTES ON THE POEMS: BOTH SCIENTIFIC AND PERSONAL

Most of what we know about what lies below comes from farming, engineering, and science. Think about it: except for going caving, finding out about the Under often requires us to dig, disturb, and destroy what is there. Even scientific methods can be invasive and change underground habitats while they record. Perhaps poetry and imagination can add to the exploration without moving anything except our minds and hearts.

UNDER: The underground roots of this green planet (along with the vital ocean, of course) are the heart of all life here. Scientists have instruments that can record the crunch and munch and movement even when the human ear can't hear it.

UNDER THE HOUSE: Even before houses had pipes, cables, and wires, the basement was where folks stored stuff, like old trunks or root vegetables.

SEEDS is about the simple—yet complicated—act of vegetation growth. **CORNY CONVERSATIONS** wonders about recent scientific studies of corn roots. It seems they emit sounds that can't be heard by the human ear alone, but *can* be recorded. There are other plants, like fennel, that also apparently make sounds. Are they gossiping, telling stories, complaining? We have no idea—yet.

THUNDER UNDERGROUND: Scientists have drilled down to drop miniature microphones below earth. They report that beetles and bugs make creaking noises (stag beetle larvae), clicking (cicadas), roaring (various bugs mating), and of course munching; the sounds of eating are everywhere. Who knew!

OH, TO BE AN ANT: Ants do have many-chambered "cities" and haul dirt four times their weight. Whether they are truly "never still" is debatable, but they sure seem that way.

EARTHWORM: As I write nonfiction poems, I come upon odd and amazing facts; for example, earthworms simultaneously crawl through the dirt and make the walls of their passages, spreading a kind of oil there. For me, learning these things is an added bonus.

MOLE EATS and **VELVET**: Moles really do have a larder of their favorite food—earthworms—though probably it's never full enough for comfort. Close up, a mole's coat looks like well-rubbed old velvet.

SUBWAY: When I was a child, I lived in New York City. My apartment house was on 97th Street and Central Park West, right over the subway. It growled and rumbled at night like some great animal in its den. I used to lie in bed imagining it, not a scary creature but a comfortable, well-tamed beast.

UNDER THE CITY: TWO VIEWS: As a city child, I was taught about how the mammoth subway system had been built. I knew the underground intimately because I rode a subway to ballet lessons on my own from the time I was ten.

THREE THINGS I KNOW ABOUT THE ROOTS OF TREES: Atilla, called "the Scourge of God" by the people of Europe, was the leader of the Hun empire of Asia. He built one of the most feared armies in the world (known as "the hordes"). His mounted warriors galloped across Austria, Germany, and northern Itay, crushing more modern nations under their hooves.

LOST CITY: To understand who we are today, we need to unravel the mystery of yesterday ("the ancient knot") by digging into the past. So, archaeologists dig up the remains of settlements, towns, and cities and study those places of habitation, literally from the ground up.

PIRATE TREASURE: The very first book I published was about pirates—women pirates—*Pirates in Petticoats*. Three hundred books later, I am still fascinated by them. I have a silver "piece of eight" pirate treasure. It hangs on my charm bracelet.

NOTES FROM SOME OLD FOSSILS: These are only three of the ways fossils are created (in ancient seas where we find them in old sandstone; in mud and tar pits such as those in La Brea, California; or encased in volcanic outpourings as happened in the ancient city of Pompeii). There are others which, with research, you could discover by yourself.

MAGMA POOLS: Magma is molten (1300–2400 degrees Fahrenheit—that's hot!) or partly molten rock found beneath the surface of our planet, often in chambers that feed into volcanoes. When it emerges from volcanoes, it's called lava and cools into a rocky substance.

TECTONIC PLATES: This is the rocky under-surface of our planet, which is broken up into about a dozen different "plates" that have shifted around through the earth's ages so that sometimes we find the same fossil evidence thousands of miles away and on different continents.

EARTH QUAKE: When there are very large earthquakes awful and strangely wonderful things can happen, often at the same time. Buildings fall, lives are lost, but mountains rise and new landscapes emerge.

UNDERGROUND RIVERS: We can see some underground rivers in caves, but there are thousands more we cannot see.

SPELUNK: "Spelunking" is the word for "going caving" (U.S.) or "potholing" (Britain)—exploring caves for fun, not scientific study. Humans have loved caves from earliest times: for shelter, for escape, for mining. Only in the last couple of centuries has caving become a sport, with its own equipment and lights.

UNDER: *Where we all end./And we all start*. We humans are part of the beating heart of the Earth. We grew up here. We end here, *ashes to ashes*, as it is said. But there is at least one other way to read the last two lines: That we started with these poems, then are led on to further explore the idea of the Under, before coming back to read the poems again, flushed with new knowledge, new factual grounding (ha!), and a new appreciation for what lies beneath our feet.